The Robert Tonner Story

UPDATE 2002

First edition/First printing

To purchase additional copies of this book, please contact:
Portfolio Press, 130 Wineow Street, Cumberland, MD 21502
877-737-1200

Betsy McCall™ is a trademark licensed for use by Gruner & Jahr Printing and Publishing Co. ©2000-2002 Gruner + Jahr USA Publishing. All rights reserved. Produced under license by Tonner Doll Company, Inc.

Ann Estelle by Mary Englebreit® "Mary Englebreit" is a registered trademark of Mary Engelbreit Enterprises, Inc. ©ME Ink 2001. All rights reserved.

Tyler Wentworth® is a registered trademark of the Tonner Doll Company, Inc. All rights reserved.

Kitty Collier™ is a registered trademark of the Tonner Doll Company, Inc. All rights reserved.

Théâtre de la Mode is used under permission granted by Maryhill Museum of Art exclusively to the Tonner Doll Company, Inc.

"For Better or For Worse™" is a registered trademark of Lynn Johnston Productions, Inc. All rights reserved. Produced under license by Tonner Doll Company, Inc. http://www.fborfw/com

Cloudland™ is used under permission granted by Shelley Thornton to the Tonner Doll Company, Inc.

Library of Congress Control Number 2002108467
ISBN 0-942620-60-7

Project Editor: Krystyna Poray Goddu
Associate Editor: Robert Haynes-Peterson
Design & Production: Tammy S. Blank

On the front cover is Tyler Wentworth® Manhattan Nights/On the back cover is Ann Estelle: A Good Book
Cover photos by Robert Hansen-Sturm

Printed and bound in Korea

The Robert Tonner Story

UPDATE 2002

Portfolio Press

Acknowledgements

For their enthusiastic and expert help in the preparation of this book, grateful thanks go to Tom Courtney and Nancy Shomo of the Tonner Doll Company.

We would like to express appreciation to Robert Hansen-Sturm of Storm Photography in Kingston, New York, for his excellent photographs of all the dolls, including most of the Transformed Tonners. We thank artists Alessandra White, Sherry Housely, Helen Kish and Heather Maciak for contributing photos of their Transformed Tonners and collector Megan Kasden for photographing Nancy Wiley's Transformed Tonner.

We are also grateful to the Tonner enthusiasts whose photos of the 10th anniversary celebration and the fashion shows helped illustrate those sections.

We also wish to acknowledge John Vanden-Heuvel for his original design of *The Robert Tonner Story: Dreams and Dolls*, upon which the design of this book is based.

Contents

A Letter from Robert 6

10th Anniversary Celebration 7

The Fashion Shows: 2000-2002 10

The Transformed Tonners....................................14

The Dolls 26

  Tiny Betsy McCall 26

  14-inch Betsy McCall 33

  Mary Englebreit Collection 42

  Tyler Wentworth 52

    Théâtre de la Mode 68

  Kitty Collier 72

  For Better or For Worse 80

  Cloudland Playdolls 82

  Collectibles 84

  Exclusives and Specials 86

Dear Friends:

In all the years of my doll art career, one of the most thrilling moments was when Portfolio Press approached me, in 1999, with the idea of a book on my years as a doll artist and manufacturer. I always felt that books were written about others—certainly not about me. They believed that the body of work I had produced up to that time was substantial enough to warrant a book—so who was I to argue?

And now, they've decided that so much has developed over the past two years that an update is in order. I am delighted to work again with my friends at Portfolio Press to bring you, in book form, all that has transpired in the two years since the publication of *The Robert Tonner Story* in 2000.

Dolls are my passion, and as my company grows more and more creative opportunities come my way. I am able to see a vision all the way through to the end product, which is, for the most part, done just as I envisioned. The dolls created between 2000 and 2002 reflect that vision. The Tyler Wentworth line has grown and matured; she has truly set a new standard of quality for the dolls we produce. My beloved Betsy McCall is still a favorite of mine and, I hope, for the collectors, as well. In the course of the past two years I have been lucky enough to work with Lynn Johnston of "For Better or For Worse" fame, Mary Engelbreit, and the model and television personality, Emme. I took my company in a new direction in working with Shelley Thornton, a doll artist I truly admire, to create the Cloudland Playdolls. Of course, I always enjoy designing my own Kitty Collier line. I loved working with the great artists of the National Institute of American Doll Artists (NIADA) on their charity project, the Transformed Tonners. (The entire collection of these dolls is shown in this book, beginning on page 14.)

So, turn the pages and see what we've been up to over the past two years. I hope you enjoy looking at my dolls even half as much as I enjoy making them.

Robert Tonner

Top: My good friend Lynn Johnston, creator of the comic strip "For Better or For Worse," came with me to the IDEX show in January 2002. **Above left and above:** Our prototype of a full-figured fashion doll, based on the model and television personality, Emme, created a big stir at Toy Fair in February 2002, especially when Emme herself visited our booth. Look for our line of Emme dolls and fashions before the end of this year.

10TH ANNIVERSARY CELEBRATION

When it came time to celebrate the company's 10th Anniversary in 2001, Robert pulled out all the stops. Robert, Company Coordinator Nancy Shomo and collector Jo Ellen Brown of Plano, Texas, who served as Convention Registrar, began planning the four-day event (May 3-6) more than a year in advance. The result was a sell-out crowd of 400, who came away with memories to last a lifetime.

Special guests such as Ginnie Hofmann, who drew the Betsy McCall paper dolls for *McCall's* magazine for years, and Lynn Johnston, creator of the comic strip, "For Better or For Worse," added to the festivities. Congratulatory letters from Lynn and from Ann Estelle's creator Mary Englebreit were included in the Convention Journal, which was also filled with stories by Scott Baver, articles by seminar presenters, and sketches by Robert.

Such an event does not happen without the hard work of volunteers. Before the official opening of the convention, Robert formally thanked his fifty volunteers with an invitation-only gathering, at which he conveyed his personal gratitude for each person's expenditure of time and energy, and then presented each volunteer with a Tyler Wentworth doll dressed in a gold silk and lace version of Standing Ovation. Each doll's face painting had been hand-detailed by Robert, and all of the couture ensembles had been made in-house. The presentation of the

doll was emotional for all, for few had ever received such an expression of gratitude. And it was well earned, for in the days that followed, Robert and the volunteer team put on one of the most memorable events of the doll industry.

Workshops, seminars and exhibits filled each day. Attendees could learn to repaint Tyler, decorate a coat and dress for Betsy McCall, create a smocked frock, doll shoes or a

Above: Robert's family joined him for the 10th Anniversary Celebration. **Left:** Models from Chicago's Ford Agency pose backstage with "Tyler" at the Saturday evening banquet's fashion show.

Top: One of Robert's special guests was his friend, Ginnie Hofmann, one of the illustrators of the original Betsy McCall paper dolls. **Above right:** Betsy McCall Spring Luncheon, limited to 350. **Above far right:** Ann Estelle Time for Tea, limited to 350. **Right:** Picnic Marni, limited to 400. **Far right:** Betsy's Perfect Birthday (10-inch porcelain), limited to 350.

Mary Englebreit greeting card. They could get behind-the-scenes insights from Tonner Design Director Molly Baver or a private viewing of the world of "For Better or For Worse" from artist Lynn Johnston. Competitive exhibitions, a sales room and a raffle room gave convention-goers plenty to admire—and wish for—all weekend long.

Individual events were planned for each of five of Robert's most beloved dolls: Betsy McCall; For Better or For Worse's April; Mary Englebreit's Ann Estelle; Kitty Collier and Tyler Wentworth. Souvenirs, dolls, favors and table settings were designed to bring a unique touch to each event. For events such as Betsy's Spring Luncheon and Marni's Picnic, a lunch theme set the tone. However, Marni's Picnic was a virtual theme as the event took place in the evening; picnic baskets and gingham together with bright lighting and cheerful music helped conjure up the look and feel of a daytime picnic. The souvenir doll was Picnic Marni, limited to 400 pieces, which came with her own lunchbox. Betsy's Spring Luncheon was more formal, and featured an exhibit of original Betsy McCall illustrations by Ginnie Hofmann. Ginnie spoke with convention-goers about illustrating America's original sweetheart, and the challenges she encountered as the decades pro-gressed. The souvenir doll was Betsy McCall Spring Luncheon, limited to an edition of 350.

Ann Estelle's outdoor tea party drew the attendees to the hotel's bridal pavillion tent where, dressed in their finest teatime bonnets (some silly and some vintage), they enjoyed a whimsi-cal party. The centerpieces at each table were Mary Englebreit teapots and the tables were set with Englebreit teacups at each place. Ann Estelle Time for Tea, wearing gloves and a large pink bow in her hair, limit-ed to 350 pieces, was the souvenir doll.

Evening events that honored the two characters most pivotal in the rise of the Tonner Doll Company were the highlights of the Tonner Anniversary Celebration. Betsy McCall's Birthday Celebration was a grand birthday party of ice cream, cake, and favors. Pastel hues of pink and lavender were carried out in the banquet's decor while Betsy McCall records played, singing birthday wishes to the spry fifty-years-young Betsy. A 10-inch porcelain Betsy's Perfect Birthday, limited to 350 pieces, was the souvenir.

Tyler's Romance Banquet was sheer elegance. Each table had rose bouquets, custommade for the event. A fashion runway was placed in the center of the banquet room to afford equal viewing pleasure to each attendee. As Robert and the models from Ford Agency worked behind the scenes to add the last touches to the scheduled Fashion Show, romantic music filled the air, creating an aura of formality and glamour. This was the only viewing of all of Tyler's fashions to date, including couture clothing that had previously been seen by a very limited audience. When it came to open the souvenir Tyler Romance doll, limited to 500, collectors mar-

veled over Tyler's newest look of brunette curls spilling over her shoulders. The embroidered pink gown of satin and chiffon drew accolades from all.

To close the convention, Robert and his team held a going-away Kitty Collier Brunch on Sunday morning. Drawing for raffle prizes was the main excitement during this event. The Kitty Collier Country Club Brunch doll, limited to 350, wearing a pale-blue embroidered dress, with coordinating hat, gloves and pearls sang of a fresh spring day—which, indeed, it was.

As attendees said goodbye, it was clear that the weekend events, filled with such thorough attention to every satisfying detail, would stay in their memories for a long time. It had been an extraordinary celebration, one befitting the occasion. Seldom does one celebrate a ten-year anniversary.

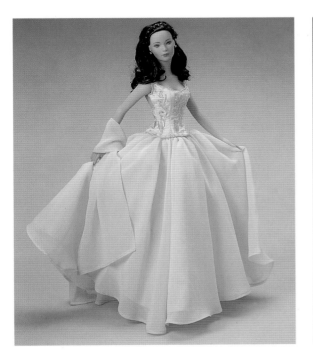

Above: Tyler Standing Ovation, limited to 50. **Far left:** Tyler Romance, limited to 500. **Left:** Kitty Collier Country Club Brunch, limited to 350.

THE FASHION SHOWS 2000-2002

Launching the Tyler Wentworth Collection wasn't just a new entry into the world of fashion dolls, it was also the realization of Robert's dream to work once

again—but on his own terms, this time—in the passionate melee known as 7th Avenue. To bring Tyler and her clothing to full-size life on the runway, Robert turned to his extensive background at Bill Blass and other fashion houses. New York's Fashion Week usually coincides with Toy Fair, and Robert found the crossover between his two worlds irresistible. He planned an elegant show to open the 2000 American International Toy Fair in New York City, treating his retailers and other special guests to an evening of New York fashion at

his own alma mater, Parsons School of Design. The first show, with its blend of character fantasy and runway reality, was the talk of Toy Fair, ensuring that it would become a much-awaited annual event.

Creating the full-scale clothing that takes Tyler's miniature world to reality is the primary focus. Calling upon his fashion-industry-trained design team, Robert takes on the task of elevating Tyler's miniature couture ensembles to human-scale. Some of the gowns cost thousands of dollars to replicate. The first year, Cashmere Noir, a beautifully tailored black cashmere winter coat, required the finest cashmere to support the silhouette Robert had designed. Fashion Design Weekly, a gown of aubergine lace with beaded accents, had to be entirely hand-beaded. In 2001, Standing Ovation, a pre-beaded pink silk delight, required a great deal of hand-finishing to complete its elaborately constructed column. Attention to details such as these make couture the art form that it has been for centuries.

To financially support each fashion show (costs can soar to as high as $70,000), Robert creates a limited-edition Tyler Wentworth outfit to be sold during the event. Market Week, limited to 1,000 pieces, in 2000, was chic in the form of a faux-leopard print skirt with a black belted wool jacket. In 2001, Prêt à Porter, limited to 500 pieces, drew upon the popular school-girl theme, pairing a pleated wool skirt and argyle sweater with black faux-leather accessories. In 2002, Cosmetics Campaign, limited to 550, exhibited a red leatherette jacket and black jeans with Tyler's Cosmetics Campaign logo printed on the miniature tee

2000

shirt. (See page 90 for photos of these dolls.)

Robert truly shines as a host when it comes to the souvenir packages. The first and second year, attendees were presented with miniature sweaters for their Tyler dolls. The 2000 sweater was pure cashmere in fashionable black and the 2001 sweater was an over-sized powder-blue cable knit. In 2002, Robert surprised attendees with a set of four Tyler lapel pins, each bearing one of the faces from the Cosmetics Campaign theme, which is based on the four seasons, as well as a full-size version of the tee-shirt worn by Tyler.

The Tyler Wentworth Fashion Show is planned in keeping with the theme of each year's collection and carefully orchestrated to create the energy and aura of a current-day fashion show. It has always been a crowd pleaser, drawing standing-room-only crowds each year.

Clockwise from left: A model wearing Premiere Pink poses next to her doll-size counterpart; a sketch of the ensemble is in the background; on the runway, a model shows off Manhattan Music Awards while another models Russian Renaissance; at the end of the first successful show, Robert Tonner and Tyler Wentworth take their bows to great applause.

2001

Clockwise from above right: Behind the scenes, a board showing photos of all the outfits for the show indicates the order in which models and outfits will make their appearance; the model wearing Chicago Sophisticate takes to the runway, showing both front and back of this elegant gown and stole; the model wearing The Look of Luxe pauses on the runway; a smiling Cover Girl Esmé poses next to the doll wearing the matching gown; at the show's end, Tyler Wentworth escorts a life-size Betsy McCall, celebrating her fiftieth birthday, down the runway; Tyler, with the models showing off her designs behind her, accepts applause and flowers after the show; a model dressed in the sophisticated Champagne and Caviar poses on the runway.

2002

Clockwise from inset, far left: the model wearing Papillion takes her walk down the runway; a dark-haired model shows off the black velvet 1950s-inspired evening gown called Manhattan Nights; the model wearing Dinner with Regina poses on the runway while the doll in a miniature version of the ensemble can be seen in the accompany-ing exhibition; the show's finale features all of the models in their cropped Cosmetics Campaign tee shirts and low-waisted jeans, exhibiting the show's theme.

THE TRANSFORMED TONNERS

In the continuing spirit of charitable giving that has characterized his career, Robert, in 2000, enlisted the participation of his fellow member artists of the National Institute of American Doll Artists (NIADA) in a fascinating fundraising endeavor. He donated an unclothed American Model to each artist, who then transformed the doll into a unique piece of art, wigging, making up, costuming and, in some cases, actually altering the body, into a figure that reflected their artistic vision. The completed thirty-nine dolls were displayed at the 2000 NIADA annual conference in Chicago, and then auctioned on eBay between August and October of that year. The dolls raised a total of $25,329, all of which was donated to the Craft Emergency Relief Fund (CERF), the American Foundation for AIDS Research (AMFAR) and NIADA. The complete collection of Transformed Tonners, an extraordinary exhibition of international artistry, is presented on the following pages.

Clockwise from top left: The doll's face reminded Richard and Jodi Creager of Shirley McClaine in the movie, *My Geisha*, so they created "Geisha." Her kimono and obi are of unique printed cotton, and her shoes are fabric and hand-carved wood. The face is hand painted. Stephanie Blythe transformed Felicity into the "Queen of the Fairies," fitting her with a silk charmeuse princess dress and a silk robe trimmed with flowers and Swarovski crystals. Her crown is fashioned from antique fabric flowers and she is accompanied by three original resin fairies, dressed in antique fabric flower petals. Mirren Barrie dressed Felicity in silk broadcloth with a gold lamé bodice and train, accented with antique braid. Her evening coat is chiffon with a lamé round collar and bat-wing sleeves. **Opposite page:** "Bird Woman," by Akira Blount, wears a handmade mask of air-dry clay, colored with acrylics and pencil. Curly willow twigs emanate from her head. She has carved wooden shoes and a skirt made of Zairian fabric, decorated with tortoise-shell buttons.

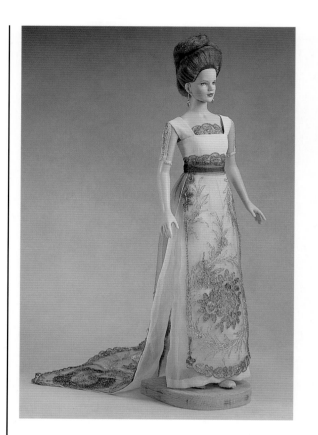

Clockwise from top left: Antonette Cely dressed Olivia circa 1910, in an Empire-waist gown and short train. The doll wears a pink satin underskirt with antique green Swiss lace over it, and has a period hairstyle and shoes. Norway's Marlaine Verhelst made her doll, "No More Frogs," a princess. She wears a double skirt with long sleeves under a paperclay bust. She has a hand-painted mask and four frogs crouch at her feet. June Goodnow's "Apache Maiden" wears a printed cotton dress trimmed with rick-rack, and a soft leather trimmed tunic. She's been re-wigged, and given a headband and woven burden basket. **Opposite page, clockwise from top left:** Kyoko Nakanishi of Japan dressed her elegant doll in traditional handmade Washi paper. Annie Wahl transformed Olivia into a Native American maiden from the Black Feet nation. Her dress, inspired by a photo, is a 1930s tanned deerskin dance dress, embellished with handmade dentalium shells, 300 cut beads, and a fringed leather band. Leggings and moccasins are of Black Feet design. Austrian artist Sylvia Natterer made "Second Skin" by coating the model with Tibetan paper, transforming a young woman into one the artist says is nearer her own age. Natterer included a signed-and-dated hang tag of her own with the doll. "Hathor," Connie Smith's creation, is the Egyptian goddess of life, fertility and beauty, embodied as a cow. Smith also transformed the paper that lines the doll's box with Egyptian hieroglyphics and paintings. Alessandra White, an apprentice of Lisa Lichtenfels, gave her doll a gray chiffon dress and mohair wig. She stands on a granite base and is accompanied by a soft-sculpture dragon.

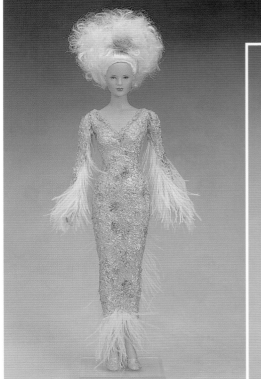

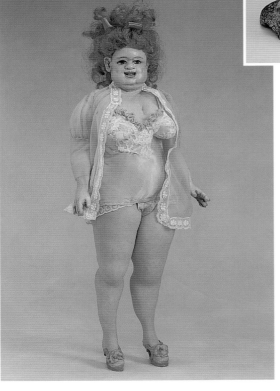

Clockwise from top left: German artist Axel Lucas created "Goldie" with feathers and gold fabric, restyling her hair. She has matching gold shoes. "Maiden Princess from a By-gone Age," by Dianna Effner transforms Regina from a "sophisticated lady with a cool, indifferent gaze into a virgin princess." Effner repainted the face, replaced the wig, and dressed the doll in a silk brocade and velvet gown with antique gold metallic trim. Her underskirt is silk and metallic crinkled gauze. JoEllen Trilling transformed Tonner's slim-figured doll into a voluptuous sixty-something portrait, using batting and nylon stocking. The fabric was stitched, painted and glued. **Opposite page, clockwise from top left:** Dan Fletcher costumed "Japanesque" in a kimono, corset and bloomers all made from Washi paper, reminiscent of the Japan-influenced paintings of European and American artists in the late 1800s. Her hair is decorated with silver and red hairpins and combs. Also evoking the 1800s, Chris Chomick and Peter Meder created a truly amazing transformation with "Olivia-Mechanical Movements Automaton." The head and arms move, powered by a wind-up key. Alaskan artist Mary Ellen Frank clad Sophie in hand-stitched leather and fur. She wears a "kuspuk" (parka) of dyed suedes, trimmed in ermine and fox. Her mittens "mukluks" (boots) are sheared calf, deer and ermine.

Above: Sherry Housley's doll wears a full-length char-treuse crushed-velvet gown with antique gold lace ruffle, gold metallic tri-point shawl and jet and gold beads. Her shoes are leather with gold detail, and she wears an antique heart-shaped necklace and gold bead earrings. **Right:** In "Strange Flower," Helen Kish turned the head, torso and hands of Tonner's doll into a 31-inch blossom of paper, antique black lace, beads and jewelry. The petals are silk chiffon and handmade paper with real leaves imbedded in them. **Opposite page, clockwise from top left:** Kathryn Walmsley's "Jester" is dressed to attend the First Quad Annual Fool's Ball in a bi-color linen camisole, silk jacket and beaded skirt, and thigh-high velvet hose with platform shoes. She wears long velvet fingerless gloves, and carries a Cernit one-of-a-kind jester companion. Her hair was bound in locks reminiscent of a jester's hat. British artists Lynne and Michael Roche dressed their doll in a kimono-style hand-knitted jacket over a natural dyed straight wool skirt. The multi-colored jacket is a splendid variation on the classic British look. Gail Lackey's doll wears a dress and shoes made from vintage bro-cade, and is adorned with a vintage fluffy maribou stole and tons of faux pearls. Her hair is finished off with a vin-tage hair piece. Inspired by a Lucille gown, "1915 Gown" by Donna May Robinson, has an overskirt of taupe chif-fon, and an underskirt lined with gold silk to match the thread woven into the French ribbon on the bodice. She wears an Austrian crystal necklace and earrings. **Opposite page, inset:** "Pearl and Lynx," by Dorothy Allison Hoskins, wears a silk dress hand-beaded with pearls and lined in gold tulle. The top has open-back laced shoulders banded in lynx. Her hair is embellished with a bead cap with gold tulle and a pearl spray halo.

Clockwise from top left: Patti Hale dressed her doll, "Barefoot in the Park", in a chic black-and-white ensemble. The doll, standing on a small base, walks two poodles. Charlene Westling's beauty wears a gown of bias-cut silk that swirls into a wide skirt. Her shoulder piece is of the same fabric with a gold thread design. She wears gold loop earrings and handmade gold slippers, and her hair is bound with gold ribbon. Nancy Wiley has transformed her model into one of her trademark pannier dolls, in which the pannier-style skirt is transformed into a backdrop for a small, resin marionette. **Opposite page, clockwise from top left:** Jo Stafford copied one of her own 1960s outfits, complete with black silk underwear. She constructed the satin dress and coat to match the originals, and paired the ensemble with leather shoes. Scott Gray re-wigged his doll and removed the legs, transforming her into a mermaid. Four layers of transparent antique fabric alternate with metallic fabric on her gown. 1940s hat veiling gives the illusion of scales. Charles Batte's "Lady Iris Goes to the Embassy Ball - The Highlight of the London Social Season" wears a 1914 evening gown of lace over chiffon. Her hair is wrapped in a feathered turban, and her handmade shoes are black-and-gold silk brocade. Margaret Finch's doll wears an evening gown of antique silk brocade draped in front to reveal the green lining. A stiff golden gauze ribbon creates a bustle effect, and emerald earrings complete the look. Marta Finch-Kozlosky's transformed doll wears a clinging LBD (little black dress) with a wire-edged bottom and thin straps. Her ruby and gold earrings are made from materials from the collection of Dorothy Heizer, owned by Marta and Margaret. She also has a tiara and ruby navel jewelry.

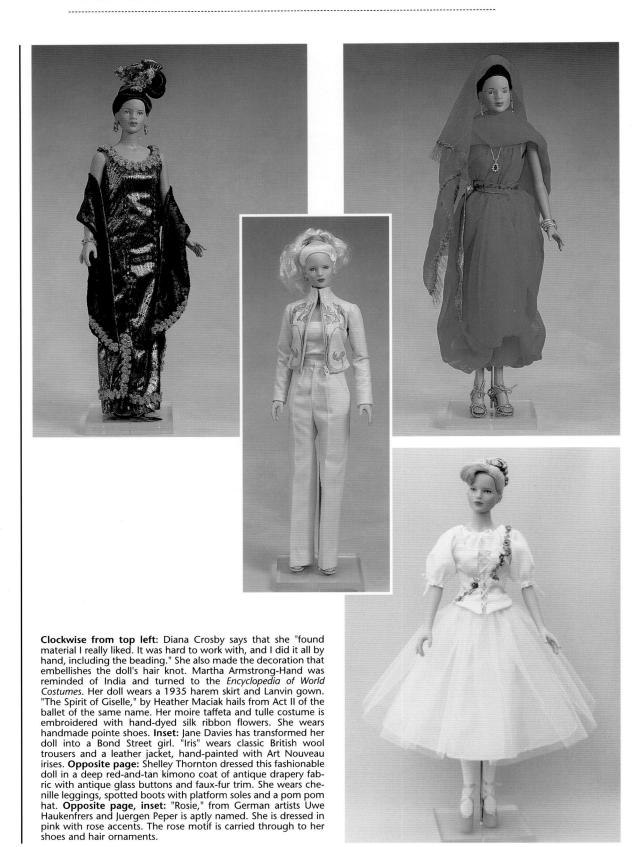

Clockwise from top left: Diana Crosby says that she "found material I really liked. It was hard to work with, and I did it all by hand, including the beading." She also made the decoration that embellishes the doll's hair knot. Martha Armstrong-Hand was reminded of India and turned to the *Encyclopedia of World Costumes.* Her doll wears a 1935 harem skirt and Lanvin gown. "The Spirit of Giselle," by Heather Maciak hails from Act II of the ballet of the same name. Her moire taffeta and tulle costume is embroidered with hand-dyed silk ribbon flowers. She wears handmade pointe shoes. **Inset:** Jane Davies has transformed her doll into a Bond Street girl. "Iris" wears classic British wool trousers and a leather jacket, hand-painted with Art Nouveau irises. **Opposite page:** Shelley Thornton dressed this fashionable doll in a deep red-and-tan kimono coat of antique drapery fabric with antique glass buttons and faux-fur trim. She wears chenille leggings, spotted boots with platform soles and a pom pom hat. **Opposite page, inset:** "Rosie," from German artists Uwe Haukenfrers and Juergen Peper is aptly named. She is dressed in pink with rose accents. The rose motif is carried through to her shoes and hair ornaments.

THE DOLLS

Tiny Betsy McCall

Above left: Betsy McCall Goes to the Theatre, 8 inches, hard plastic, 2001; **Top left:** Betsy McCall's Sundress, 8 inches, hard plastic, 2001; **Above left:** Betsy McCall Makes a Wish (outfit only), 2001; **Left:** Betsy McCall has a Happy Holiday, 8 inches, hard plastic, 2001; **Opposite page top:** Betsy McCall Takes a Ballet Class, 8 inches, hard plastic, 2001; **Opposite page left:** Introducing Betsy McCall - Tosca, Blonde, Brown, each 8 inches, hard plastic, 2001

Above right: Betsy
McCall Writes a
Letter to Grandpa
(outfit only), 2001;
Above far right:
Betsy McCall Goes
Sleigh Riding
(outfit only), 2001;
Right: Betsy
McCall
Sails a Boat,
8 inches, hard
plastic, 2001;
Far right: Sweet
Dots (outfit
only), 2002

Far left: Betsy Visits the Ranch, 8 inches, hard plastic, limited to 2,000, 2002; **Left:** Pretty & Perky (outfit only), limited to 1,500, 2002; **Below:** All American Gift Set includes one hard plastic 8-inch doll, four outfits shown, and two shoe pairs, limited to 1,000, 2002

Above right: Betsy Loves Bunnies, 8 inches, hard plastic, limited to 2,000, 2002; **Right:** Rose Cotillion, 8 inches, hard plastic, limited to 2,000, 2002; **Far right:** Lunch in the City (outfit only), limited to 1,500, 2002

Above: Piano Recital, 8 inches, hard plastic, limited to 2,000, 2002; **Left:** Shopping with Mommy, 8 inches, hard plastic, limited to 2,000, 2002

Above right:
Sunny Days (out-
fit only), limited
to 2,000, 2002;
Right: Bedtime
Stories,
8 inches, hard
plastic, limited to
2,000, 2002;
Far right: Betsy
McCall Wardrobe
Trunk (doll not
included), 2002

14-inch Betsy McCall

Above: Betsy Style 1960s, 14 inches, vinyl, 2001; **Left:** Betsy Style 1950s, 14 inches, vinyl, 2001

Above right:
Betsy Style 1970s,
14 inches, vinyl,
2001; **Right:**
Betsy Style 1980s,
14 inches, vinyl,
2001; **Far right:**
Betsy Style 1990s,
14 inches, vinyl,
2001; **Opposite
page:** Betsy
McCall as
Cinderella, Sandy
McCall as Prince
Charming, each
14 inches, vinyl,
2001

Above right: All Dressed Up (outfit only), 2002; **Right:** Duffle Coat Darling, 14 inches, vinyl, limited to 1,000, 2002; **Far right:** Just Betsy (basic doll), 14 inches, vinyl, 2002

From left:
Beecharmer Drew, 2002; Beecharmer Betsy, 2000; Beecharmer Barbara, 2002; each 14 inches, vinyl, limited to 250

Above: Purple Pajamas (outfit only), 2002;
Right: Leaf Peeper (outfit only), 2002

Above: Snowflake Sweetie, 14 inches, vinyl, 2002; **Left:** Sandy as Peter Pan, 14 inches; Linda as Tinker Bell, 10 inches; Betsy as Wendy, 14 inches; each vinyl, limited to 500, 2002

Above right: Swiss Miss (outfit only), 2001; **Right:** Simply Spring (outfit only), 2001; **Far right:** Betsy McCall Native American, 14 inches, vinyl, 2001

Above left:
Linda McCall
Travel Time,
14 inches, vinyl,
2001; **Left:**
Raincoat (outfit
only), 2001;
Far left: Linda's
Party Dress
(outfit only),
2002; all three
part of Linda
Travel Time Set,
2002

Mary Engelbreit Collection

Above right: 18-inch Calendar Girl, vinyl, limited to 1,000, 2002; **Right:** Camp Breit Light, 10 inches, vinyl, limited to 1,000, 2002; **Far right:** Cherry Dress (outfit only), limited to 1,000, 2002

Left: Caroling Girl, 10 inches, vinyl, 2002; **Far left:** Mary Engelbreit Trunk, 2002; **Below:** Toybox, Bed, Bedside Table (dolls not included), 2002

Above right:
Baking Cookies,
10 inches, vinyl,
limited to 1,000,
2002; **Right:**
Classic Sailor, 18
inches, vinyl, 2001;
Far right: Basic
Gracie, 10 inches,
vinyl, 2002

Above left: Red Velvet Holiday, 10 inches, vinyl, limited to 1,000, 2002; **Left:** First Place, 10 inches, vinyl, limited to 1,000, 2002; **Far left:** Scotty Skirt and Saddle Shoes, 10 inches, vinyl, 2002

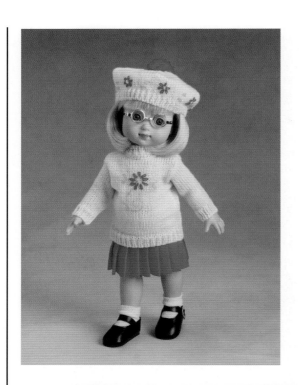

Above right: Well Ain't You Somethin' (outfit only), limited to 1,000, 2002; **Right:** Table & Chairs (dolls and tray not included), 2002; **Opposite page:** The Queen of Everything, 10 inches, vinyl, limited to 1,000, 2002

Above right:
May Flowers,
18 inches, vinyl,
2001; **Right:**
Aloha Ann Estelle,
10 inches, vinyl,
2001; **Far right:**
Prima Ballerina,
10 inches, vinyl,
2001

Above far left:
Field Guide,
10 inches, vinyl,
2001; **Above
left:** Firecracker
Annie, 10 inches,
vinyl, 2001; **Far
left:** A Good
Book, 10 inches,
vinyl, 2001; **Left:**
Mother's Day,
10 inches, vinyl,
2001

Above right: Basic Sophie, 10 inches, vinyl, 2001; **Right:** Basic Georgia, 10 inches, vinyl, 2001; **Far right:** Let's Skate, 10 inches, vinyl, 2001

Above left: Ride 'Em Cowgirl, 10 inches, vinyl, 2001; **Left:** He Sees You When You're Sleeping, 10 inches, vinyl, 2001; **Far left:** Trick or Treat, 10 inches, vinyl, 2001

Tyler Wentworth

Please note: While Tyler is classified as a vinyl doll, she is actually composed of vinyl and hard plastic.

Above and right: Tyler Signature Style Brunette, 16 inches, vinyl, 2002; **Right:** Drafting Table and Stool, Design Essentials, Dress Form, 2002

Above left: Champagne and Caviar, 16 inches, vinyl, limited to 2,000, 2001; **Left:** The Look of Luxe, 16 inches, vinyl, limited to 2,000, 2001; **Far left:** Black-and-White Ball Sydney, 16 inches, vinyl, limited to 2,000, 2001

Above right:
Metro Chic (outfit only), limited to 2,000, 2001;
Right: Chill Chasers (outfit only), limited to 2,000, 2001;
Far right: Standing Ovation, 16 inches, vinyl, limited to 1,500, 2001

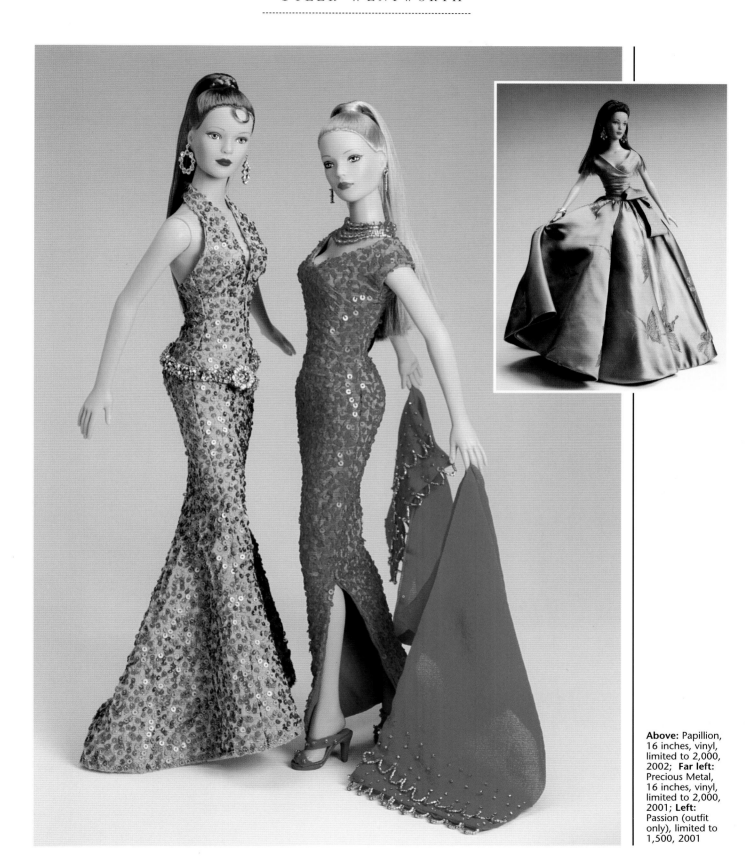

Above: Papillion, 16 inches, vinyl, limited to 2,000, 2002; **Far left:** Precious Metal, 16 inches, vinyl, limited to 2,000, 2001; **Left:** Passion (outfit only), limited to 1,500, 2001

Above right: City Tweed (outfit only), limited to 1,500, 2002; **Right:** Little Luxuries (outfit only), limited to 1,500, 2002; **Far right:** Florentine, 16 inches, vinyl, limited to 1,500, 2002

Above left: Midnight Garden, 16 inches, vinyl, limited to 1,000, 2001; **Left:** Boston Bound, 16 inches, vinyl, limited to 2,000, 2001; **Far left:** Dinner with Regina (outfit only), limited to 1,500, 2002

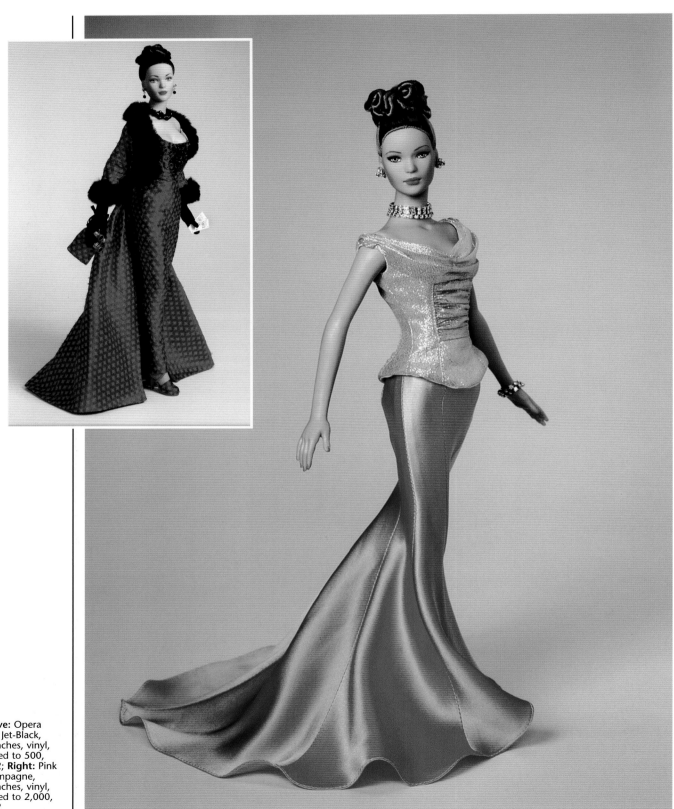

Above: Opera Gala Jet-Black, 16 inches, vinyl, limited to 500, 2002; **Right:** Pink Champagne, 16 inches, vinyl, limited to 2,000, 2002

Above: Capital Investment, 16 inches, vinyl, limited to 2,000, 2002; **Left:** Madison Afternoon Gift set (doll and outfits), 16 inches, vinyl, 2002

From right: Dolls—Ready-to-Wear Spring (basic doll), shown full-length; Ready-to-Wear Fall (basic doll); Ready-to-Wear Summer (basic doll); Ready-to-Wear Winter (basic doll); each 16 inches, vinyl, 2002; **Above right:** Deluxe Wardrobe Trunk (doll not included), 2002; **Inset:** Basic Wardrobe Trunk (doll not included), 2002; **Far right:** Summer Shoe Essentials, 2002; Winter Shoe Essentials, 2002

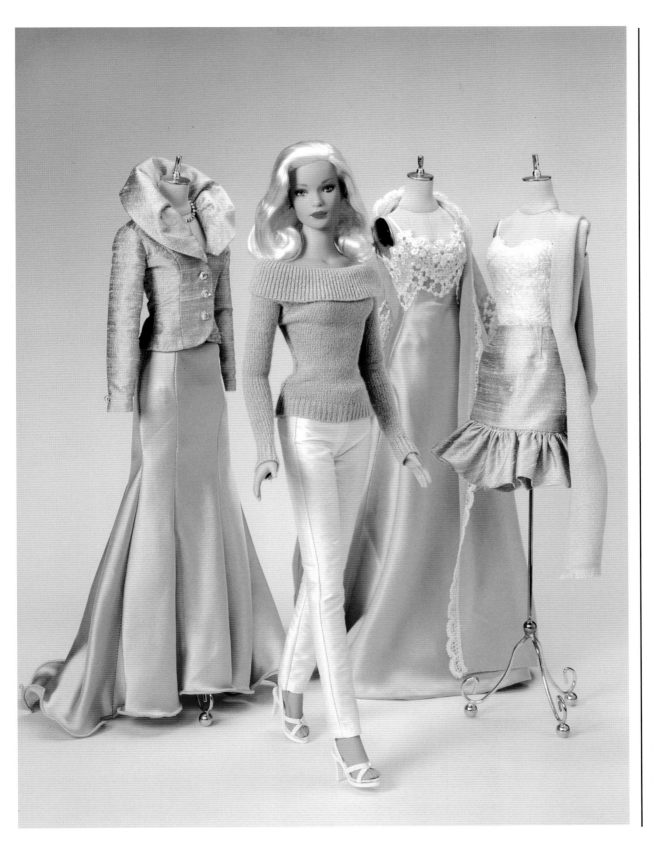

Sweet Indulgences
Gift Set, (doll
and outfits, but
dress forms
not included),
16 inches, vinyl,
limited to
1,000, 2002

Above right: New England Excursion (outfit only), limited to 1,500, 2002; **Right:** First Appointment Mei Li, 16 inches, vinyl, limited to 1,000, 2001; **Far right:** Patron of the Arts (outfit only), limited to 1,500, 2002

Above: Tailleur Classique; **Far left:** Pretty Young Thing; **Left:** Uptown Paradise, each outfit only, limited to 2,000, 2001

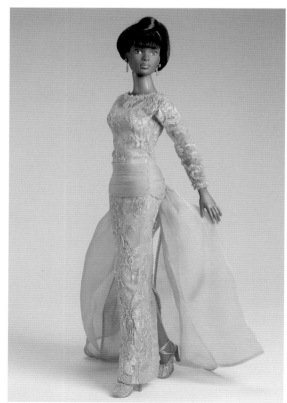

Above right: Wild Orchid Esmé, 16 inches, vinyl, limited to 2,000, 2002; **Above far right:** Basic Esmé, 16 inches, vinyl, 2001; **Right:** Urban Sport Esmé, 16 inches, vinyl, limited to 500 (outfit only limited to 3,000), 2002; **Far right:** Cover Girl Esmé, 16 inches, vinyl, limited to 2,000, 2001

Left: Sheer Beauty Mei Li, 16 inches, vinyl, limited to 2,000, 2002; **Top:** Embassy Dinner Mei Li, 16 inches, vinyl, limited to 2,000, 2002; **Above:** Weekend Retreat (outfit only), cashmere edition limited to 1,000, wool edition limited to 3,000, 2002

Top: Sydney Chase and Black- and-White Ball Sydney Chase, 16 inches, vinyl, (final production version), 2001; **Above:** Sydney Chase, 16 inches, vinyl, 2001; **Right:** Sheer Glamour Sydney, 16 inches, vinyl, limited to 2,000, 2002

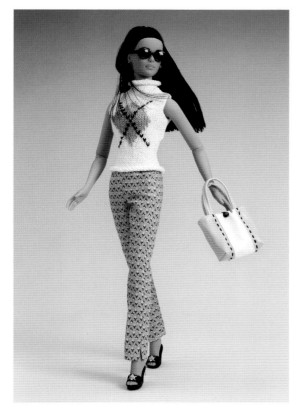

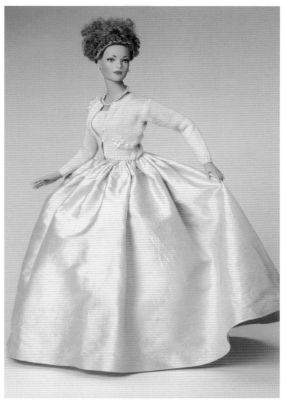

Above far left: Lake Shore Drive (outfit only), limited to 1,500, 2002; **Above left:** Premiere Pink (outfit only) limited to 3,000, 2000; **Left:** Weekend in Washington Gift Set (doll and outfits), 16 inches, vinyl, limited to 1,000, 2001. (Note: This gift set with a blonde version of the doll was made as an exclusive for Dollmasters of Annapolis, Maryland, in 2001, and limited to 250.)

Tyler Wentworth

Théâtre de la Mode

Please note: This collection of haute-couture is inspired by the 1945 showing of the Théâtre de la Mode in Paris, now housed at the Maryhill Museum of Art in Goldendale, Washington.

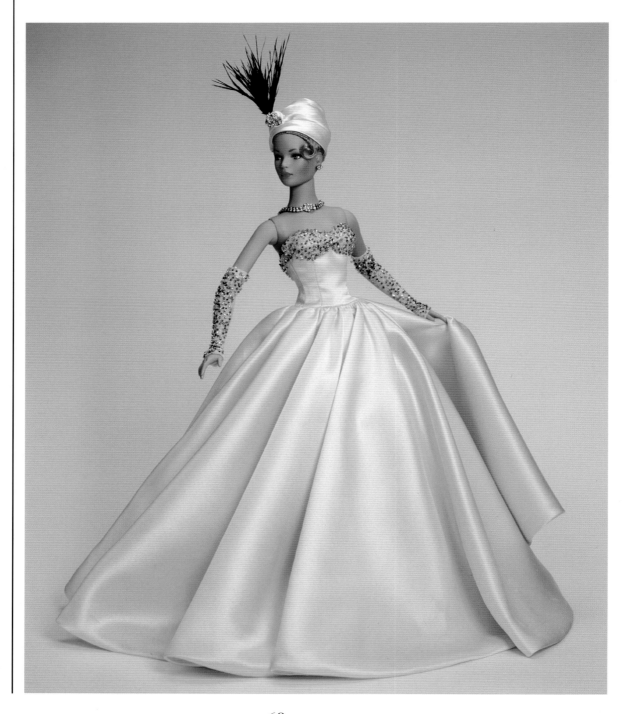

Reflet d'Argent
16 inches, vinyl,
limited to 3,000,
2002

Above: Le Petit Ensemble Noir, 16 inches, vinyl, limited to 3,000, 2002; **Left:** Soir de Fête, 16 inches, vinyl, limited to 3,000, 2002

Above:
Longchamp
Fleuri, 16 inches,
vinyl, limited to
3,000, 2002;
Right: Fleurs du
Mal, 16 inches,
vinyl, limited to
3,000, 2002;
Opposite page:
Framboise Robe
du Grande Soir,
16 inches, vinyl,
limited to 3,000,
2001

Kitty Collier

Summertime Swing, 18 inches, vinyl, limited to 1,500, 2002

Left: Basic Redhead, Blonde, Brunette, each 18 inches, vinyl, 2002; **Above:** Kitty Shoes, 2002

Above: Lunch with the Ladies (outfit only), limited to 1,000, 2002; **Right:** Sapphire Sashay (outfit only), limited to 1,000, 2002

Above: Femme Fatale, 18 inches, vinyl, limited to 1,500, 2002;
Left: Year of the Dragon, 18 inches, vinyl, limited to 1,500, 2002

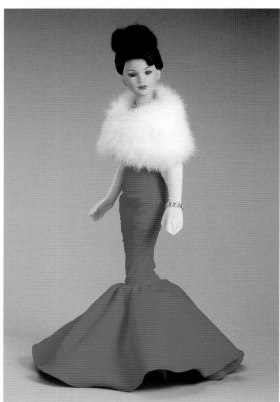

Above right: First Class, 18 inches, vinyl, limited to 1,500, 2002; **Above far right:** Parfait Promenade (outfit only), limited to 1,000, 2002; **Right:** Picture Perfect, 18 inches, vinyl, 2001; **Far right:** Scarlet Glamour, 18 inches, vinyl, 2001; **Opposite page**: Lilac Cotillion (Kitty Couture), 18 inches, vinyl, limited to 1,000, 2002

Above: Hot Spots (outfit only), 2001; **Right:** Down Mexico Way (outfit only), 2001

Above far left:
Enchanté (outfit
only), 2001;
Above left:
American Beauty,
18 inches, vinyl,
2001/2002;
Far left: My
Blue Heaven,
18 inches, vinyl,
2001/2002;
Left: Patio Party
(outfit only),
2001

For Better or For Worse

Above right: Dressy April, 10 inches, vinyl, 2002; **Right:** April, 10 inches, vinyl, 2001; **Far right:** April Sport Shorts, 10 inches, vinyl, 2002

Above far left: April Flowers, 10 inches, vinyl, 2001; **Above left:** Dance Class, 10 inches, vinyl, 2001; **Far left:** April's PJs (outfit only), 2002; **Left:** April Puddle Jumping (outfit only), 2002

Cloudland Playdolls

Above: I Can Fly (outfit only), 2001; **Right, from left:** Genevieve; Lulie; Nora; each 24 inches, vinyl head, hands, feet with cloth body, 2001

Left: Slumberland (outfit only), 2001; **Top:** Tea Party (outfit only), 200; **Above, from left:** Hattie, Sylvie, each 24 inches, vinyl head, hands, feet with cloth body, 2002

Collectibles

Red Riding Hood,
18 inches, vinyl,
2002

Above: Baking
Gingerbread,
18 inches, vinyl,
2002; **Left:** Alice,
18 inches, vinyl,
2002

Exclusives and Specials

Right: Tyler Wentworth High Tea, Santa Fe Doll Art, Albuquerque, New Mexico, April 15, 2000, 16 inches, vinyl, limited to 350; **Above far right:** Vienna Opera Ball, Tyler Wentworth's Spring Collection, Portland, Oregon, March 31- April 2, 2000, 16 inches, vinyl; limited to 400; **Far right:** Shamrock (outfit only), Collector's United, Nashville, Tennessee, March 2000, limited to 100

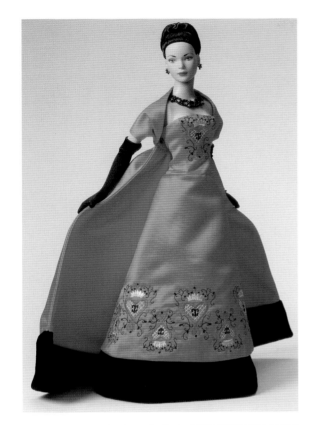

Above far left: Queen of Hearts, Collector's United, Nashville, Tennessee, March 2002, 16 inches, vinyl, limited to 300; **Above left:** Kitty Collier Centerpiece, Collector's United, Nashville, Tennessee, March 2002, 18 inches, vinyl, limited to 50; **Far left:** Vienna Waltz, Collector's United, Nashville, Tennessee, March 2001, 16 inches, vinyl, limited to 350; **Left:** Little Bo Peep, Collector's United, Nashville, Tennessee, March 2002, 8 inches, hard plastic, limited to 300

Above right: Palm Beach Nights, Walt Disney World Teddy Bear and Doll Show, Orlando, Florida, October 19-21, 2000, 16 inches, vinyl, limited to 500; **Right:** Sydney Chase, Focus on Fashion, United Federation of Doll Clubs (UFDC), Atlanta, Georgia, August 9, 2001, 16 inches, vinyl, limited to 500; **Far right:** Chicago Sophisticate, UFDC, Chicago, Illinois, July 17, 2000, 16 inches, vinyl, limited to 500; **Opposite page:** Kitty Collier's Dress Shop, Walt Disney World Teddy Bear and Doll Show Auction, Orlando, Florida, October 19-21, 2000, 18 inches, vinyl, one-of-a-kind

Above right: Market Week (outfit only), Tyler Wentworth Collection, New York, New York, February 12, 2000, limited to 1,000; **Above far right:** Prèt â Porter (outfit only), Tyler Wentworth Collection, New York, New York, February 10,2001, limited to 500; **Right:** Cosmetics Campaign (outfit only), Tyler Wentworth Collection, New York, New York, February 9, 2002, limited to 550; **Far right:** Fashion Show Specials (sweaters only) Tyler Wentworth Collection, New York, New York, black cashmere cardigan-February 12, 2000, powder blue pullover-February 10, 2001, souvenirs

Far left: Manhattan Music Awards (dressed doll version), Italian Doll Festival, Bologna, Italy, November 2001, 16 inches, vinyl, limited to 60; **Above left:** Masquerade, Modern Doll Convention, New Orleans, Louisiana, October, 2001, 16 inches, vinyl, limited to 325; **Left:** La Femme Chic, Paris Fashion Doll Festival, Paris, France, March 2001, 16 inches, vinyl, black dress, limited to 300; La Femme Chic Centerpiece, red dress, limited to 20

Above right: Cover Girl Tyler, 16 inches, vinyl, made in three versions: Brunette-Tonner Doll Collectors Club, Doll & Teddy Bear Expo East, August 24-26, 2001, Washington, D.C., limited to 100; Redhead-FAO Schwarz, Chicago, Illinois, May 2001, limited to 100; Wheat Blond, (not shown) FAO Schwarz, St. Louis, Missouri, June 2001, limited to 100; **Right:** All that Glitters, FAO Schwarz, Mall of Georgia, August 2001, gift set, limited to 100; **Far right:** Santa Tyler, NBC's *Today Show* appearance, New York, New York, November 2001, 16 inches, vinyl, one-of-a-kind; **Opposite page, from left:** Ensemble d'Or, Galeries Lafayette, Paris, France, September 2001, 16 inches, vinyl, limited to 100; Cygne Noir, Paris Fashion Doll Club, Paris, France, 2001, 16 inches, vinyl, limited to 100

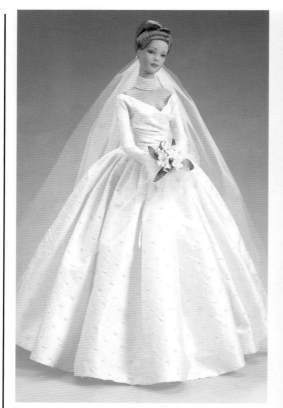

Above right: Tyler Wentworth Bride, *Here Come The Bride Dolls* written by Louise Fecher, published by Portfolio Press, 2001, 16 inches, vinyl, one-of-a-kind; **Right:** Fashion Show Finale, *Here Come the Bride Dolls* gift set with book, 2001, 16 inches, vinyl, limited to 500; **Far right:** Manhattan Nights, *The Robert Tonner Story Update 2002* gift set with two books, published by Portfolio Press, 2002, 16 inches, vinyl, limited to 750

Far left: Opera Gala Esmé (variation), Happily Ever After, Philadelphia, Pennsylvania, 2001, 16 inches, vinyl, limited to 30; **Above left:** A Little Night Music, Corbett's Collectibles, Maple Shade, New Jersey, 2000, 16 inches, vinyl, limited to 1,000; **Left:** Nights in White Satin, Corbett's Collectibles, Maple Shade, New Jersey, 2001, 16 inches vinyl, limited to 500

Clockwise from top left: Millennium Betsy, Back to the Future Betsy McCall Convention, Mesquite, Texas, May 2000, 14 inches, vinyl, limited to 300; Tenth Anniversary Jane Doll, Tonner Doll Collectors Club, 2001, 14 inches, vinyl, limited to one production run; Betsy Florida Day, 30th Anniversary of the Fort Meyers Doll Club, Fort Meyers, Florida, April 2002, 14 inches, vinyl, limited to 300; Betsy Celebrates America the Beautiful, Doll & Teddy Bear Expo East, Washington, D.C., August 18-20, 2000, 14 inches, vinyl, limited to 75; Millennium Marni, Tonner Doll Collectors Club, 2000, 8 inches, hard plastic, limited to one production run